This book belongs to

Copyright © 2023 by Jenni Pearce.

All rights reserved. No part of this book may be used or reproduced in any form whatsoever without written permission except in the case of brief quotations in critical articles or reviews

Note for readers :

This book should be read at a steady, calm pace to ensure the listener is in a calm and relaxed state.

The adventure then unfolds to allow their mind to take on the positive principals of the story.

Text and illustrations by Jenni Pearce

ISBN 978-1-7392833-1-5

www.thecouragetochoose.com

First Edition: February 2023

The Magical Gift

Jenni Pearce

I'd like to take you on a magical journey.

On this journey you can learn how to use your amazing mind to help you.

As you go on your adventure you will be adding new information, just like programming a computer or robot.

You might want to close you eyes or keep them open to look at the pictures, whichever feels most comfortable for you.

A good way to prepare for your adventure is to make sure that you are nice and relaxed. You can start this by taking in a long, slow breath.

Calmly breathing in through your nose, then slightly open your mouth and release all of the air from your body in a big, long, low, deep sigh, as though you are blowing a kite and trying to make it go high into the sky.

As you breath gently you start to feel nice and relaxed. You can just let anything that you are thinking about disappear, and float away like a big balloon, just floating up and away.

As you watch it floating away can you see what colour it is ?

Is it your favourite colour ?

The balloon is floating away, floating away, high above the clouds.

Perhaps you can blow away some more balloons.

Now think about your hands, and gently wriggle your fingers making them feel all loose and floppy.

Just notice them for a moment and in your imagination slowly count to 3.

1 2 3

Make sure those fingers are all wriggled out and nice and relaxed.

Do they feel all floppy ? If not just wriggle them a bit more until they feel loose and floppy like squiggly spaghetti

Think about your legs and feel them go loose and floppy, letting go of any uncomfortable feelings

Relax and let go, imagine them like squiggly spaghetti

As you grow more relaxed it feels like you are floating on a big soft cloud.

Can you feel it like a big marshmallowy cloud all squishy underneath you.

It feels so soft and warm and comforting.

You now feel safe and relaxed and are ready to begin your adventure.

Imagine that in front of you is a magical hot air balloon.

You know that it's magical because of all of the the wonderful colours on it that dance and sparkle in the sunlight.

You get into the basket and it feels nice and safe.

You can see that there are flags on the basket and they begin to sway and move as the balloon slowly lifts up, gently into the air.

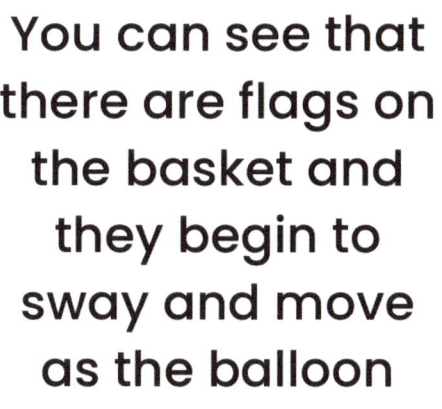

You can feel yourself being lifted up as the balloon goes higher and higher into the beautiful blue sky.

Up over mountains and clouds.

When you look down you can see the trees, fields and houses below.

You're going gently higher, you can feel yourself floating now.

All of things below you are growing smaller as they get further and further away.

Looking down you can see that in the very middle of the forest is a beautiful tall castle.

It looks so inviting that you decide to float down, and take a closer look.

You are floating down to the beautiful castle below.

As you gently float further down you become more and more relaxed.

Your magical balloon lands softly on a clump of fresh, sweet-smelling grass and you are so excited to explore the castle.

Ahead of you is a path of stepping stones, edged with beautiful colourful flowers, leading to the castle.

You see a sign which says that you can make a wish if you want someone with you and in an instant they will be there.

It could be somebody that you know for real or in your imagination.

You make your wish and as you do sparkles appear making a glittering shower and whoever you have wished for is suddenly there.

You set off towards the castle, following the stepping stones path.

You stop and admire the flowers on the way as you take in their beautiful shapes and colours, and they smell so wonderful.

You continue on your way and through the door ahead of you which opens allowing you to enter the castle.

As you go into the castle you are amazed at the size of the room ahead. There are many doors for you to open, enter, and explore.

You and your guest look around, and go through the door ahead of you.

In the room is a large wooden table with freshly made food. You see all of your favourite things. You look at the scene in front of you and try some of the delicious foods.

You notice the sun gleaming through the windows. Beautiful colours are reflecting all around the room

On the table in front of you, you can now see a large gift that is wrapped in beautiful paper and a big bow. It is wrapped in sparkly paper that changes colour as the light catches it.

You see there is a label with your name on it.
You unwrap the box and open the gift very carefully.

Inside the gift is a rainbow coloured cloud. It is so beautiful and mysterious, yet you're not quite sure what it is or what it does.

The person who is with you explains that it is a magical cloud.

They have spent a long time looking for this special gift. They tell you that it has magical powers that can help you do many wonderful things.

They take the gift out of your hands and gently lift it over your head. You feel very excited as a shower of glittering stars come floating down over you, and feel ready to go ahead and do the things that you were once uncertain about.

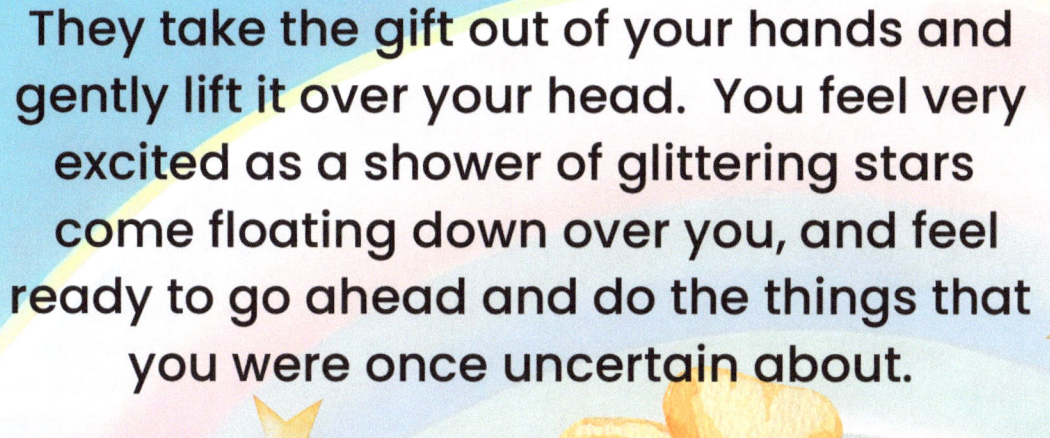

It doesn't matter what this could be as your magical mind will know what this needs to be.

You wonder through the rooms seeing all the wonderful new things in front of you and you feel so happy and relaxed.

Before long it is time to leave the caste and you go you find your way back to the door you came in through.

You see the magical balloon there waiting for you and you climb on board.

As you travel back you know that you now have more confidence than you thought possible, and know how good you will be at the things you enjoy, or at trying new things.

It feels like the best feeling in the world

You'll find that you feel more and more confident about everything from now on.

You can see everything from a whole new angle.

The gift that was given to you will stay with you always.

And now imagine putting your new confidence to the test. Imagine yourself doing whatever it was you were once worried about doing.

Just think about something you would like to do, and imagine the rainbow coloured cloud just above you, showering you with feelings of confidence once again.

You are feeling really proud of yourself.

You find yourself smiling more and feeling much happier than you ever did before.

Whenever you want to feel this way again you can.

All you need to do is imagine your rainbow cloud showering you with wonderful confident feelings.

These feelings of confidence grow stronger and stronger day by day and night by night.

Even when you are sleeping your mind will be helping you.

Other books available in **The Magical You** series

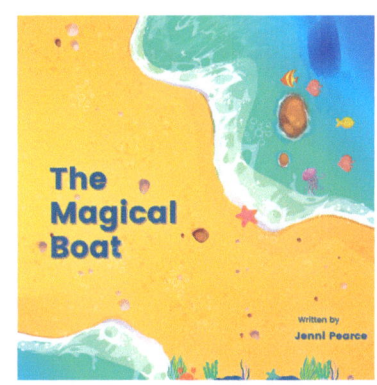

www.ingramcontent.com/pod-product-compliance
Lightning Source LLC
Chambersburg PA
CBHW041229040426

42444CB00002B/104